THE
SUPREME
COURT

Illustrated by Leonard Everett Fisher

WILLIAM MORROW AND COMPANY
New York

1962

THE
SUPREME
COURT

EQUAL·JUSTICE·UNDER·LAW

72982

BY

GERALD W. JOHNSON

TO

A<small>NN</small> K<small>ATHRYN</small> <small>VAN</small> <small>DEN</small> H<small>ONERT</small>

Contents

Illustrations

THE SUPREME COURT

What the Supreme
Court Does

I N THE CITY of Washington, near the Capitol
and the Congressional Library, stands a great
white marble building that everyone admires, but
that many people prefer to admire from outside. If
they enter, they step lightly, almost on tiptoe, and
speak softly; for this is the building of the Supreme
Court of the United States, and wise men don't play
games with the Supreme Court.

Wise men don't play games with any court, for
if you speak or act disrespectfully while the court is
sitting, the judge can put you in jail and keep you
there until you have apologized. But if a man feels
that he has been treated unfairly by the court, he
can appeal to a higher court and have his case ex-
amined. Not in the Supreme Court, though. It *is* the
highest court, and from its decision there is no appeal. So a wise man is doubly careful not to bring
down its wrath upon his head.

The power and dignity of the Supreme Court give many of us a feeling that it is somehow farther apart from ordinary people than either of the other two branches of government, the executive and the legislative. To be sure, the Presidency is an office of great dignity, and the President has enormous power. Congress is a dignified body, and in some ways more powerful than either of the others, because Congress, as the saying is, "carries the purse." When the other branches need money, they can get it only from Congress.

Yet both the President and Congress seem closer to us than the Court. For one thing, we have elected the President and the members of Congress, but we did not choose the judges. For another, and much more important reason, we understand what the President and Congress are doing, because they constantly explain it in our own language. The Supreme Court also explains its actions in any important matter, but it uses the language of the law, which is so different from ordinary talk that people who have never studied law find it hard to understand. This gives us a feeling that the Court is farther away from us than any other part of the government; we know that it is very grand and very powerful, but we feel that it is very strange and a little bit scary.

So visitors to Washington look at the great marble

temple respectfully, but most of them prefer to stay outside.

We all have to live under the laws that Congress makes. The President is the national leader in time of peace, and the commander in chief in time of war. They are in the news every day. We know what they are doing, and we think we know why they are doing it. We can keep up with them.

The Court is different. A great deal of its work is of a kind that people simply can't get excited about unless they are mixed up in the case, which few of us are. Did the ABC Company, in making a certain gadget, infringe a patent right that belongs to the XYZ Company, and, if so, how much damage was done? Really now, who cares? The two companies care, of course, but to you and me it makes not the slightest difference who turns out the gadget. We don't know anything about patent rights, and if we tried to follow the ins and outs of the case, we should wind up utterly confused.

So we don't. We leave it to the judges and the lawyers, who are paid to understand such things. Most of us have enough to worry about with matters that we do understand. So we admire the Supreme Court, but, like the visitors to Washington, from the outside.

Up to a point, this makes sense. The law is a profession that can be mastered only by many years

of study. You and I don't have to know it, because
there are plenty of lawyers who have spent their
lives studying it, just as doctors have studied disease.
A man who would go into court without a lawyer is
as foolish as a sick man who would refuse to call a
doctor.

But there is a point at which it no longer makes
sense to pay no attention to the Supreme Court, for
it is a great deal closer to us than we sometimes
think. The law is not an end in itself. We did not set
up our enormous legal system just to give work to
lawyers and judges. It has a purpose, and we understand the purpose, all right. The purpose of the law
is to serve justice.

Justice means letting every man have what is
rightfully his, and no more. If you will think about
it for a moment, you will see that that covers a lot
of ground. In fact, it just about covers the whole
earth; which is why the law, whose purpose is to
serve justice, is an enormous system and so complicated that there isn't a man alive who knows all
about it.

When anyone, no matter whether he is a school-
boy or the President of the United States, is denied
something that he thinks is rightfully his, he is unhappy. As a rule he is angry, too. It happens to all
of us sometimes, so we all know how he feels. Most
of the time it happens about something not really

important, so we don't worry too much. If it is something big, however, then the person who suffers injustice feels about as bad as anyone can feel.

Suppose, then, most of the people in a nation begin to feel that they have no hope, or very little hope, of getting justice even in the biggest and most important things. It would be a nation of very unhappy and very angry people, certainly not a pleasant place in which to live. Some men, having no hope of getting justice from the government, would start out to get it for themselves. There would be fighting and killing and robbing everywhere. Nobody could live in peace and safety.

Now the Supreme Court of the United States is the main stem of the American system of justice, so the idea that it is something far away from us, with which we have little or nothing to do is as wrong as an idea can be. It is so close to us that if it fell into the hands of wicked men, or foolish men, our liberty would be in danger, our property would be in danger, and we couldn't be sure that even our lives would be safe.

So an American who wishes to understand his country cannot afford to look at the Supreme Court from the outside only. Because the United States is a great and powerful country, it is a great and powerful court; one that we like to think is the greatest in the world. Even so, it doesn't belong to the nine men who make it up and whom we call the justices—a Chief Justice and eight Associate Justices. It belongs to the people of the United States. The business it attends to is the people's business, and when the Court is in session — *sitting* is the word generally used—its doors are open and anyone may listen to what is going on, as long as he keeps quiet. It is lawful for you, whoever you may be, to walk into the big building and, unless all the public seats are already taken, into the courtroom itself. Probably you will not understand much of what you hear, but nobody will prevent your listening.

Not all of us can go to Washington and actually sit in the courtroom, but let us take a look at the Court as it appears today to the eyes of a visitor who makes up his mind to go into the building.

When you first enter, you may be astonished to see how simple is the room in which the most powerful court in the world sits. You face a long desk on a dais only a little above the floor level. Behind the desk are nine high-backed chairs. In front of it, on the floor level, is a plain reading desk, and at each side is another desk, facing the long one and smaller than it. A little farther away are two tables, one on each side, with chairs facing the long desk. The two smaller and lower desks to left and right are for the clerk of the Court and the marshal. The tables are for the lawyers on the two sides. Then comes a railing and, behind that, rows of seats for the public. That is all.

But make no mistake — plain as it is, that room is magnificent. The draperies that look like red velvet *are* red velvet, and of high quality. The furniture does not have a mahogany finish, it *is* mahogany, and of the best in the world. Each of the nine chairs behind the long desk was specially built to the measurements of the justice who is to occupy it, and has his name on a small metal plate attached to the back. Everything in the room, while plain in design, is of the very highest quality.

The Chief Justice sits in the middle chair, with four Associate Justices on each side. The chair at the Chief Justice's right hand is that of the justice who has been longest a member of the Court; the chair on his left belongs to the justice next in seniority. The others follow in the same order, so that the newest Associate Justice is always at the extreme left. When a justice dies, or retires, and a new one is appointed, attendants take the chair at the left end of the desk and transfer it to the right end, putting the new man's chair in its place. But when a Chief Justice is appointed, he sits in the middle chair from his first day on the Court.

The clerk keeps the official record of the proceedings, makes out the orders of the Court, receives petitions addressed to the judges, keeps the docket

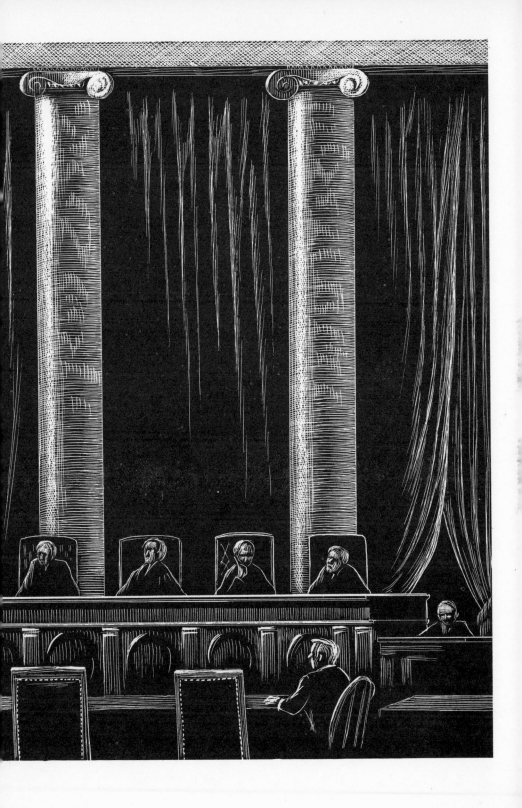

—that is, the list of cases to be heard—and handles all the documents connected with the cases. The marshal keeps order in the courtroom, is the manager of the building, and bosses the attendants and other people who work there. He also opens and closes each session of the Court.

The opening of the Court usually interests visitors, because the marshal, or a deputy under his orders, acting as court crier, recites a formula that has been recited in English-speaking courts for hundreds of years. It begins with a word that is not English at all, but Norman French, from the days of William the Conqueror. It is *oyez,* meaning, "Hear ye!" In the Supreme Court room, precisely at noon, a signal is given and everyone rises to his feet. The Chief Justice enters, followed by the eight Associates, all in black robes. When they have taken their places, the Chief Justice signals the crier, who instantly shouts, "Oyez, oyez, oyez! All persons having business before the Honorable, the Supreme Court of the United States, are admonished to draw near and give their attention, for the Court is now sitting God save the United States and this Honorable Court!" Then everybody sits down and business begins.

From the spectator's standpoint the proceedings are likely to be dull, for the Supreme Court compels everyone concerned to stick to the business in hand, without any foolishness. The lawyers on both sides have already written out their arguments and handed them to the clerk of the Court, who has passed them on to the justices. These arguments are called *briefs* — ironically, since a brief in a Supreme Court case is never short, and some of them are long enough to make a large book. But at that, the lawyer usually wants to add something to his brief, or to explain something in it, so the Court allows him to make an oral argument.

Back in the old days it was considered quite correct for such an orator as Daniel Webster to make the courtroom resound to his high-flown eloquence, but not now. Today no smart lawyer ever thinks of making an oration to the Supreme Court. He simply steps up to the reading desk and talks in a quiet, conversational tone. Frequently one of the justices will interrupt with a question, and sometimes quite a debate follows before the point is made clear. At two o'clock the Court recesses for lunch, opens again at two-thirty, and adjourns for the day at four-thirty.

But when the Court adjourns, the heavy work of the justices has only begun. Each takes a copy of the briefs back to his private office, reads them, compares them, studies them. With a secretary taking notes, and a law clerk fetching and carrying books and looking up references to decided cases—one floor of the building is given up to a big law library open to all lawyers, with a smaller one for the justices only—he tries to make up his mind which side is more nearly right.

Then on an appointed day the nine justices assemble in a conference room, to which nobody else is admitted, and there they have it out as to what the decision of the Court shall be. "We fight like cats and dogs," one member of the Court told a newspaper reporter. At any rate, after everyone has had his say, the Chief Justice calls for a vote. Usually the newest justice votes first, and the Chief Justice last. If as many as five agree, their decision becomes the decision of the Court. The Chief Justice then appoints one to write the opinion. If they all agree, he usually writes it himself. The written opinion explains to the world why the Court decided as it did, and lower courts and lawyers all over the country will thereafter refer to it as the law on that particular subject, so it has to be written carefully in order that there may be no mistake as to what it means.

When the decision is written, the justices have another conference and go over it, line by line, looking for spots that might be misunderstood. They change words and phrases. They cut out a sentence here, and add one there. Sometimes they rewrite the whole thing. When at last it satisfies them, the man who wrote it originally reads it in open court on the next decision day, usually a Monday.

Two things, however, must be borne in mind. In the first place, easy cases never get to the Supreme Court, except in quite unusual circumstances. If a State is suing another State, or if an ambassador of a foreign country is suing, or being sued, the Supreme Court takes charge right from the beginning. But other cases must be heard first by a lower court, and unless there is something very doubtful about the decision the Supreme Court will not hear the case.

In the second place, each of the nine men on the Court is, as a rule, a strong-minded man; if he had not been, he never would have been appointed. Now when nine strong-minded men are dealing with a difficult problem, it would be foolish to expect perfect agreement all the time. In fact, in important cases a unanimous decision is unusual.

Yet a strong-minded man is never convinced he is wrong simply because five out of nine men don't think as he does. Thus the minority claim the right not only to disagree, but to explain publicly why they disagree. So when the Chief Justice has assigned one man to write the decision of the Court, the ones who are not satisfied, sometimes as a group, sometimes each man for himself, write what are called dissenting opinions, and these dissents also are read in open court and put upon the record.

For the very reason that Supreme Court cases are always difficult, it is not unusual for the passage of time to show that some dissenting justice really saw the case more clearly than the majority did. Well, his dissent is on the record. The next time a similar case comes up, the justices can read it, and if they become persuaded that the dissenter was right, the Court will, as we say, "reverse itself." What was the dissent will now become the law.

That is why lawyers are accustomed to say that the truth is in the Supreme Court record. If you can't find it in the decision, you will find it in the dissent.

Decisions of the Supreme Court frequently involve corporations worth many millions, even billions of dollars. When the decision is announced, the stock of the winning corporation is likely to go up in price and that of the losing one may go down. So if a man knew in advance what the decision was going to be, he might make a great deal of money without doing any work at all, by going into the market and buying or selling the right stock, simply because others did not know about the decision. This would be unfair, so great care is taken not to let the news get out until the decision is read.

The original copy is sent to printers who work in the basement of the Supreme Court building. These men are paid by the Government Printing Office, away on the other side of the city, but once assigned to the Supreme Court they work nowhere else. They are always old and trusted employees, who can be relied on to keep their mouths shut. Even so, the whole decision is never given to any one typesetter; it is cut into short "takes" that are numbered and assigned to several men, so that each man may say truthfully that he didn't know what the whole decision was. But they seldom say it; they don't talk at all about their work. Once in a while news of a decision has "leaked," but the leak has rarely, if ever, been traced to a printer.

The Chief Justice is head of the Supreme Court, but that doesn't mean that he rules it. He has one vote, and it counts for no more than the vote of any other member. He presides in the conference room, and he names the men who are to write the decisions, but for the rest his duties are like those of the others. His salary is a little higher—$35,500 a year as against $35,000 for Associate Justices. When the Court walks in procession, he walks in front; when a new President is inaugurated, he administers the oath; and when a President is impeached, he presides at the trial, but that has happened only once. The real distinction is that he is the highest officer of one of the three branches of government; therefore he is of equal rank with the President and the Speaker of the House.

All the same, it is an exalted office, the highest professional distinction that an American lawyer can attain. It is the more honorable because in all

the years since the government was founded no Chief Justice has ever brought disgrace upon it. Some have had finer minds and been greater judges than others, but not one has been guilty of conduct that would bring his colleagues and the country to shame. There are not many courts in the world with as long a history of which as much can be said.

Of the Associate Justices only one, Samuel Chase, who served from 1796 to 1811, has been impeached. (He should not be confused with Salmon Chase, the Chief Justice right after the Civil War.) Even in his case the charge was not that he was dishonest or treasonable, but that he was too violent-tempered to be fair. The real reason was that he insisted on making political speeches from the bench, denouncing the President and the administration. This was undoubtedly foolish on Chase's part, but it wasn't a crime and the impeachment failed.

How do the Constitution and the laws make sure that the justices of the Supreme Court shall always be honest men, and usually very able men? What are the qualifications for the office? The answer is astonishing, for it is — none. The President of the United States may appoint anyone he chooses. The justice doesn't even have to be a lawyer. In fact, he doesn't have to be a man, for the President could appoint a woman.

But the appointee cannot take office until his nomination has been confirmed by the Senate. If there should be any doubt about either his character or his learning, the Senate will refuse to confirm. But it cannot then proceed to choose someone more to its liking. It must wait for the President to appoint another and, if necessary, a third, until he finds one whom the Senate will confirm. So, although the law sets no qualifications, it is practically impossible for a really crooked or ignorant man to get on the Supreme Court.

Membership of the Supreme Court of the United States changes rather rapidly. The reason is easily understood. When the President has to name a new member, he wishes to name one whom the Senate will confirm; therefore, he looks for a man with a fine reputation for honesty, knowledge, and wisdom.

But such a reputation is not made quickly. As a rule, a man must live a good many years before he becomes so eminent that people will say of him, "He ought to be on the Supreme Court." Bushrod Washington, at 36, was the youngest justice ever to sit on the Court; and some have suspected that President Adams appointed him, in 1798, as much because he was a nephew of George Washington as because of his own reputation.

This means that when a man first joins the Court he is practically always middle-aged and often elderly. Although the justices are appointed for life, few of them last as long as Oliver Wendell Holmes, who served twenty-nine years and retired at ninety-one, or John Marshall, who served thirty-four years and died at eighty. Nearly every year at least one of the nine dies or retires.

Any list of the justices, accurate when it is written, is likely to be wrong by the time it appears in a book, because some justice will probably have been replaced by another man. Below is a list of the members of the Court as they were when this was written, but the reader should check to make sure that it is still correct. It is included here mainly to show what kind of men are appointed to the Court; for although the Court may not consist of the same men by the time the reader sees this, it is pretty sure to be made up of the same *kind* of men. This, then, is the Court as it was early in 1962:

Chief Justice of the United States

Earl Warren. He was the attorney general of California and then governor of the State before he was appointed to the Supreme Court.

Associate Justices of the Supreme Court

Hugo L. Black. He was a Senator from Alabama before he joined the Court.

Felix Frankfurter. He was a professor of law

at Harvard. He is also the only member of the
Court born in another country (Austria).

William Orville Douglas. He, too, was a professor of law, at Columbia for a while, and then
at Yale.

Thomas C. Clark. He was a lawyer in Texas,
and then attorney general of the United States before joining the Court.

John Marshall Harlan. He was a judge of the
Circuit Court of Appeals in New York. It is inter-
esting to know that his grandfather, who had the
same name, also was an Associate Justice.

William Joseph Brennan. He was a justice of
the State Supreme Court of New Jersey.

Potter Stewart. He was a Federal circuit court
judge in Ohio.

Byron Raymond White. He was a lawyer in private practice, and then deputy attorney general
of the United States.

Four of the justices in this list were judges of lower
courts and were promoted to the Supreme Court. All
four, as well as the Chief Justice, were appointed by
President Eisenhower, who believed that being a
judge is a very special line of work, best done by
men who have had long experience in it. Not all
Presidents have thought so, and it is rather unusual
for as many as four of the nine justices to be men

promoted from lower courts. This is because Americans regard the Supreme Court as somewhat different from all other courts.

The Power of the Supreme Court

Every civilized nation has a high court of some kind, but the Supreme Court of the United States differs from all others in that it is more than a court. It is, in fact, one third of the government, playing an important part not only in deciding where we are today, but which way we shall go tomorrow.

Other high courts determine what the law is, and with that they are through. But the Supreme Court of the United States, not once, but many times, has determined what the law *shall be*, which in theory is the business of Congress alone.

For instance, in 1896 the Court said that it is quite all right under the Constitution to compel the railroads to carry white and colored passengers in different coaches, provided the coaches are exactly alike. This was the "separate but equal" doctrine in the case that the lawyers call *Plessy vs. Ferguson,* or, more often, just Plessy, and for fifty-eight years it was applied not only to railroads, but to many other things, including schools. Actually the Fourteenth Amendment (which is the part of the Constitution under which the ruling was made) doesn't say anything about "separate but equal," one way or the other, for or against. But some kind of rule had to be made, so when the Court said that "separate but equal" should be the law, that made it the law, at least until the Court, or Congress, or the people said something different.

Then in 1954, the Court said that as far as schools are concerned "separate but equal" will not do, because the very fact of being separate makes schools unequal. So the Court ordered what is called *integration*, that is, that all public schools shall be open to all children, no matter what their color. And that made integration the law. In neither case did Congress do anything; the Court determined what the law should be.

Just as the 1896 decision was applied to a great many things other than railroad trains, so the 1954 decision has been applied to a great many things other than schools. But racial integration is far more than something for lawyers to quarrel over in the courtroom. It changes not merely the law, but a whole social policy; it affects the lives of everybody except, perhaps, those who live in places where no form of segregation ever existed. Such places are few, for even where segregation was not the law it has often been a social custom. It has proved much harder for the Supreme Court to change custom than to change the law, and it has not entirely succeeded yet, but most of the high courts in other nations would not even think of trying.

The power of the Supreme Court is not absolute, however. If it hands down a decision that most of the people think is wrong, that decision will not stand. After a while the Court itself will reverse it; if not, Congress will pass a law reversing it; and if neither can be done, and the people continue to think the decision wrong, they will adopt a constitutional amendment that will reverse it. We usually state this principle by saying that "sovereignty belongs to the people," sovereignty being the last, highest power. But amending the Constitution is a slow and difficult process, and Congress doesn't like to fight the Supreme Court. So except when the people are very strongly of the opinion that a decision is wrong, it is correct to say that the law is what the Supreme Court says it is.

We say that Congress makes our law and the President enforces it. Yet we allow nine men — indeed, five out of nine — to say that a law passed by Congress and signed by the President is no law and nobody need obey it. We allow them to say that what they themselves said was law yesterday is not law today. Then we, the people, claim the right by amending the Constitution to say, regardless of the President, Congress, and the Supreme Court, that the law shall not be what they say it is, but what we desire it to be.

This looks like no system at all, but utter confusion. Yet the American legal system today is as sturdy as any, and a great deal stronger than most. Somehow under this arrangement we have managed to keep order, to do business, and to grow prosperous and great.

Most of us have not thought about it enough to be sure how the system works, but from the early days the American people have had one peculiar idea about the Supreme Court. Because it is the court that has the last word, for beyond it there is no appeal, Americans, including most laymen and some lawyers, have always felt that while inferior courts must be courts of law, the highest of all should be a court of justice. The difference is that when a court of law has said, "This is the law," it is finished and can say no more. A court of justice, however, must say, "This is just," and if it cannot do so because of a law, it must strike down the law.

To men with logical minds this is a dreadful idea, for it seems to leave the judges free to write their own law as they go along; and if we allow that, why

have a Congress? But the American layman doesn't
see it that way. The judges are not left free. The
Constitution limits them. But one of the six purposes
for which the Constitution was made is "to establish
justice," hence if a law plainly establishes injustice,
it defeats that purpose and, therefore, is unconstitutional.

Actually it is unheard-of for Congress to pass a
law that is frankly and rankly unjust on its face. The
cases that come to the Supreme Court involve bor-
derline acts — laws that are just when you look at
them one way, but unjust when you look at them
another. The Court's problem is to decide from
which angle they should be viewed. The rule which
it usually follows is to assume, first, that Congress
means to be just, and, second, that Congress knows
as much about the facts as the Court does. Therefore, unless those who attack it present a very strong
case, the law must be allowed to stand.

Nevertheless, some members of the Court, including some very great ones, have always felt that this
rule ignores the Court's most important duty, which
is to serve justice. These members are always inclined to strike down any doubtful law, and when
there are as many as five of them they can start up-
roars, especially if the five hold an idea of justice
that does not agree with the idea held by the majority of the people. In 1936, for example, the very ex-

istence of the Court seemed threatened when five members struck down, one after another, a whole series of laws that the people strongly approved. In 1937 one member changed sides and indignation against the Court died down, but it was a near thing.

That was exceptional, but in practically every instance when the Supreme Court declares a new law unconstitutional, or gives a new meaning to an old one — as when it reversed the Plessy decision — you will always hear someone saying that this is "judge-made law," that it is a terrible thing, that it threatens the American system of government, and that it ought not to be tolerated.

But that is far from certain. If the judges concerned are bad men, or stupid men, of course they will make bad law; if they are honest and wise, their law will be as good as any other. And judge-made law is not contrary to the American system. It is a part of the American system, made so by the way in which the Constitution was written. Judge-made law came to be because, when something had to be done and there was nobody else to do it, the judges acted. Sometimes what they did was not wise and made bad law; sometimes it was excellent. In both cases it has been tolerated, because men learned long ago that usually bad law is better than no law at all.

This much is certain: it was often by some decision of the Court, rather than by an act of Congress,

that a Constitution written in 1787 was made to fit
a situation that didn't exist in 1787. Because the old
Constitution could be made to fit new conditions, it
has not been necessary to write a new one, and today it is the oldest written Constitution in the world.

Take, for example, the steamboats in New York
harbor. In 1787 steamboats were no problem, because there were none, here or anywhere else in the
world, except, perhaps, some models that various
inventors had made, none of which worked very
well. Thus there was no reason why the Constitution
should mention steamboats, and it didn't. There was,
though, such a thing as trade among the States, and
that the Constitution did mention, saying that Congress should regulate it. This made sense, because if
it had been left to the state legislatures, each one
equal to the others, nobody would have been boss
and the rows would have gone on forever.

But in 1807 Robert Fulton put on the Hudson
River a steamboat that really would work. The New
York legislature admired it so much that it gave
Fulton and his partner, Robert R. Livingston, a monopoly, that is, an exclusive right, to operate steamboats in the waters of New York State. At first nobody objected, but after a few years other people
wanted to get into the steamboat business and did,
among them a certain Cornelius Vanderbilt, called
the Commodore, who was not only a smart business-

man, but a bold, determined fellow, not disposed to let anybody stand in his way.

On the west side of New York harbor is the State of New Jersey. The boundary line between the two states runs down the middle of the harbor. Commodore Vanderbilt, with some others, set up a company to run steam ferries from Elizabeth, New Jersey, to New York City. But as soon as the ferries crossed the line, they were in New York waters, which broke the Fulton-Livingston monopoly. So although the New Jersey legislature approved the Vanderbilt company and gave it a charter, New York held the ferries to be lawbreakers and forbade them to come in.

There followed a battle between the steamship interests that was comic in some ways, but in other ways very serious indeed. The Livingston crowd — Fulton had died before all this happened — got the New York courts to issue injunctions against the Vanderbilt crowd, and the Vanderbilts got the New Jersey courts to issue injunctions against the Livingstons, and neither paid the slightest attention to the courts of the other State. Vanderbilt crewmen were arrested when they landed in New York, and Livingston crewmen were arrested when they landed in New Jersey. There were riots when the two gangs met, and all sorts of dodges were used to beat the other side. In short, there was no law at all in New York harbor.

But in 1824 the case finally came to the Supreme Court in Washington. The Court held that while the Constitution doesn't mention steamboats, it does mention interstate commerce, and trade between New York and New Jersey is interstate commerce, which Congress shall regulate. But the New York legislature isn't Congress, so it had no right to forbid a steamboat from another state to come into New York waters. As against Vanderbilt's New Jersey company, the monopoly New York State gave to Livingston was no law at all.

The thing most worth noting about this is how easily the Court could make the old Constitution fit a new state of affairs. This was because of the way it was written in 1787. The men of that day could not foresee the steamboat, but they could foresee great changes in the country. They believed that the thirteen former colonies were sure to grow, and they thought the growth would be great and rapid. If they intended the law they were writing to last, it would have to be flexible enough to fit many and probably very important changes.

Marshall and Taney

To MOST OF US it now seems plain that when people claim that a law violates the Constitution, the Supreme Court ought to decide the matter. It seems so plain that we are surprised that anybody should ever have thought otherwise, but some people did, and quite important people, too. During Washington's two terms and John Adams' one term the question never came directly before the Court. But during Thomas Jefferson's first term it did.

The election of 1800 was the first Presidential election in which two definite political parties opposed each other, and the Republicans, led by Jefferson, beat the Federalists, led by John Adams. It so happened that Oliver Ellsworth, Chief Justice of the United States, had been sent on a special mission to France and while he was there his health broke down. He sent back his resignation, which arrived just about the time of the election, and that left the office vacant. Adams still had time to fill the job, and John Marshall, his Secretary of State, suggested one man after another. But none suited Adams, who finally appointed John Jay, a former Chief Justice who had resigned. Jay refused the offer. Then Adams said to Marshall, "I believe I must appoint you," and so it was done.

Today we read that record with astonishment. To be named Chief Justice of the United States is the highest professional honor that can be won by an American lawyer. In two ways it is a more desirable office than that of President of the United States — first, the appointment is not for four years, but for life, or until the Chief Justice chooses to retire. Second, it doesn't require so much speechmaking and handshaking. The Chief Justice lives in Washington in a house chosen by himself. He receives only such visitors, and talks only to such people, as it suits him to receive and talk to. He doesn't have to worry about Congress, or the party, or elections; it would be most improper for him to interfere in politics. Yet he, like the President, is head of one of the three branches of government. As far as official rank goes, the President and the Speaker of the House are his equals, but nobody is his superior.

But it was not so in the beginning. In the beginning, the Supreme Court was regarded as a sort of side issue, a necessary agency of the government, but not really part of it, not actually having a share in running the country. So in the early days strong and ambitious men felt that if they went on the Supreme Court they were sidetracked. Of course, it was a stately and dignified office, but if a man wanted to be somebody important in the making of the country; he was likely to regard a job on the Supreme Court as a kind of honorable retirement.

The men of 1787, in fact, thought that Congress was to be the real power in America. Most people expected Congress to become what the House of Commons now is in England. Even the Presidency was expected to be more honorable than powerful, and when Washington was elected the first President, it was as a reward for what he had already done rather than as a demand for further services.

In the same way the Supreme Court was expected to stand aside from the active work of governing. To be sure, it was to have sole possession of the judicial power, but nobody realized clearly what the judicial power was or could be. When the makers of the Constitution separated the powers of government, they didn't know exactly what they were doing. How could they? It had never been done before. It was all theory that had not been put to the test of practice, and few theories, when put into practice, work out exactly as expected.

So it is really not surprising that during its first twelve years the Court had four different Chief Justices and eleven different Associates, although at the start the whole Court consisted of only four men. Today if a man knew that he had an incurable disease that would soon affect his mind, he might refuse an appointment as Chief Justice of the United States; but it is hard to believe he would turn it down for any less compelling reason. This is a tremendous change, and it was brought about largely by one man, John Marshall. It is no wonder that he is regarded as one of the most important men in our history.

You can say that the change was bound to come, and if not through Marshall it would have come through some other man, so why call him important simply because he happened to be there? But the change was not bound to come. The Supreme Court might have taken the view that it was obliged to accept any law passed by Congress. If it had done so, we should never have had the balance of powers that many think necessary to keep the republic alive. Without that balance the United States probably would have broken apart right after the War of 1812, and almost certainly would have broken apart at the time of the Civil War. Perhaps some other man would have done what Marshall did, but perhaps not; and it is almost a certainty that nobody else could have done it as smoothly and cleverly. Figure it any way you will, John Marshall was a very great man, although a very proud and stubborn one.

There is no doubt that one of his reasons for accepting the job of Chief Justice was that in that position he hoped to get a crack at Jefferson, whom he hated bitterly although he was a distant cousin. Today even those who do not like his doctrine agree that Thomas Jefferson was one of the very great Presidents, but in 1801 John Marshall couldn't see him as anything of the kind. Marshall really believed that Jefferson was at heart a Jacobin, and the name of Jacobin then was as bad as the name of Communist today. The Jacobins were the extremists in the French Revolution of 1789, as the Communists were in the Russian Revolution of 1917.

When Jefferson was elected, Marshall had serious doubts that the republic could last for four years under such a President unless some way were found to curb him. Congress was no reliance, for the Jeffersonians had won Congress as well as the White House. The judiciary seemed to Marshall the last hope. Two years passed before he found a way to act, and then he did it so slickly that few people in the country realized what had happened.

It had to be done that way, if it were done at all. Today the Court has such enormous prestige that it is hard for us to realize that in 1803 it had little, if any. The number of its judges had been raised from four to five, but that was almost its only change. The Court had not a single soldier, not even a policeman, to enforce its decisions. The Marshal of the Court had no police power outside the building, nor does he today. The United States marshals, who do have police power, are under the President, not the Court. The President commanded the Army and Navy. Congress could declare war and levy taxes. The Court could do nothing except announce its decisions, and to announce a decision and then not be able to make it stick is to become ridiculous, as Marshall well knew. His problem was to issue a decision that the other branches would not like, and make it stick without the use of force.

He did it by a bit of legal juggling so fancy that one must know all the circumstances to appreciate it. The Federalists had been bitter about losing the election in November, 1800, and before Jefferson's inauguration, in March, 1801, they thought up every scheme they could to keep as much of the government as possible. In those days, after an election in November, the old Congress met again in December and sat until March 4. The new one did not come in until the following December. So even after the election the Federalists still had Congress, and one of their schemes was to pass a law creating a large number of new judgeships, to which President

Adams appointed Federalists. John Marshall, who was then still Adams' Secretary of State, helped the scheme along. The Jeffersonians said Congress made so many new judges that President Adams and Secretary of State Marshall sat up until midnight, March 3, 1801, getting the commissions signed and sealed, and they called the Federalists appointed to these jobs "midnight judges." Even so, Adams and Marshall did not quite finish. They got the commissions signed, stamped with the seal, and most of them sent out; but a few were left lying on the Secretary's desk and were still there when the new Secretary, James Madison, took charge the next day.

Among these was a commission as magistrate in the city of Washington issued to one William Marbury. Nobody is sure what happened to it, but it wasn't sent to Marbury, so he asked the courts to order the Secretary of State to hand it over. In the course of time — in 1803 to be exact — the matter came up to the Supreme Court. This was the famous case of *Marbury vs. Madison.*

Chief Justice Marshall wrote the decision of the Court, and it was a marvel. There are reasons for believing that it is pretty bad law — in later decisions Marshall as good as said so himself — but as a political dodge it has rarely, if ever, been excelled. It said (a) that Marbury was entitled to his commission and (b) that Secretary Madison was acting tyrannously and wrongfully in withholding it, but (c) that the Supreme Court could not issue a writ compelling him to hand it over, because (d) the Constitution had outlined exactly what the Court could do, and no such writ was mentioned. Therefore, and here is the dynamite, (e) although the Federalist Congress in 1789 had passed a law allowing the Court to issue such writs, Congress had no right to expand the jurisdiction of the Court, hence that law was unconstitutional, null, and void. Mr. Marbury was entitled to his commission, yes, but he could whistle for it as far as the Court was concerned.

Historians are still amazed at the colossal nerve of the man. Marshall was saying that Madison had committed an unlawful act, which could not be corrected legally. Then and there he repudiated the ancient doctrine that there is no wrong for which the law does not supply a remedy. He asserted that Congress could not extend the jurisdiction of the Court to permit it to issue a certain kind of writ, but *he* could extend it by declaring a law of Congress void — an immensely greater extension than anything tried by Congress.

But see where it left the Republicans. They wanted all the midnight judges thrown out, and this decision, in effect, threw Marbury out. They couldn't object to that. They were opposed to practically everything the Federalist Congress had done, and this decision struck down one law of that Congress. They were not inclined to object to that. Yet it established the principle that the Supreme Court could declare an act of Congress unconstitutional, therefore void, thus making the Court, not Congress, the last authority on the validity of a law. At that time no court anywhere in the world claimed such authority as its own right. If any court claimed the right to nullify a law, it would make itself part of the legislative power.

Jefferson saw this immediately, and raged, but what could he do? The only way to knock out the decision would have been to impeach the whole Court, and that couldn't be done, for the Republicans did not have the necessary two-thirds majority in the Senate. Besides, many of them were so pleased that a midnight judge had lost his case that they did not want to upset the decision. So it stood, and Marshall, who never cared two straws about Marbury anyhow, made his point.

He went on to strengthen the Court's position in decision after decision, but most of the others were much sounder law than that in *Marbury vs. Madison*. For instance, there was one called the Dartmouth College case, in which Daniel Webster, as lawyer for the college, made one of his most famous orations. The point, however, was not settled by Mr.

Webster's eloquence, but by hard, clear thinking on this question: how good is a contract signed by the government if the government wants to get out of it? The Court's decision was, perfectly good. And that, too, was a new idea in law.

What had happened was that back in colonial days the king of England had given a charter to a board of trustees to set up a college in New Hampshire, to run it themselves, and when a trustee died or resigned, to elect another. That is, it was what is called a self-perpetuating board.

Time passed, and the Revolution transferred the king's authority to the State of New Hampshire. Then, fifty years after Dartmouth had been founded, lawyers for the college came before the Court complaining that the legislature of New Hampshire, desiring to take it over, had declared the king's charter void and had fired the board of trustees. They asked the Court, could a State do a thing like that?

This brought up all kinds of legal questions. To begin with, all hands agreed that the legislature now had the authority that once belonged to the king. But was the king's charter a contract? If it was, could private persons (the trustees) hold the sovereign power (the State of New Hampshire) to any agreement if the sovereign power chose not to be held? If so, could this group of private persons, who were merely trustees, not owners, of the college, claim to be injured if what did not belong to them were taken from their control? It is an old principle of law that a person who is not injured has no right to sue when a contract is broken.

The Court held that the king's charter was a contract, that the State was bound by it, and that, a trusteeship being a position of honor, a trustee was injured when dismissed without cause. Therefore, the legislature could not lawfully take over control of the college against the will of the trustees.

This decision was important to many people who cared nothing about Dartmouth College, because what the Court said of one contract was presumed to be true of all contracts. It meant a great deal to businessmen at the time, since the New Hampshire legislature was not the only one that seemed inclined to back out of contracts when it found them inconvenient. They were doing it on any excuse. Sometimes they claimed that the State had been cheated in the original deal, but sometimes they didn't even say that much. They would try to back out, because the opposition party had made the contract, or sometimes because of a quarrel between religious sects. A religious quarrel was part of the Dartmouth College case.

But you simply can't do business in a big way when people are not bound by their contracts. If a

State legislature could cancel any contract with private persons whenever it felt like doing so, then private persons could never safely do business with a State. Thus the decision that the State is bound by a contract it makes with private persons was a great relief to businessmen everywhere. Some persons growled that Marshall was depriving the States of their sovereign power, but most felt that sovereign power never gave even the king a right to go back on his pledged word, so the decision did not take from the States anything that was rightfully theirs.

That same year (1819) another case came up that was a good deal more complicated and so gave rise to much more argument. Its formal title is *McCulloch vs. Maryland*, but laymen call it the Bank of the United States case. In 1816 Congress had chartered a national bank, and endless disputing followed, because, as a matter of fact, a national bank was both a good thing and a bad thing. It was good in that it gave the government a safe place to keep its money, an agent to sell its bonds, and one central authority to issue bank notes that would serve as paper money. It was bad in that the government owned only the smaller part of the stock, could name fewer than half the directors, and so did not have full control over its own money.

At the time many thought — and some continue to think to this day — that this arrangement was all right, because the government ought not to have control of money and banking. The British government did not control the Bank of England, so why should our government control the Bank of the United States?

But others were violently opposed to allowing any one bank to have charge of all the government's money. They said it created a monopoly and that the small group of bankers who owned most of the national bank's stock could put any other bank out of business. Therefore, they tried to hamper the Bank of the United States in every way possible. Of course, most of the state banks took this view.

The opposition group had a majority in the Maryland legislature, so when the Bank of the United States set up a branch in Baltimore, the legislature slapped a heavy tax on it. The Bank refused to pay, and the suit followed. The State claimed that Congress had no right under the Constitution to charter a national bank, and if it did, the State of Maryland had a right to tax the branch doing business in the State.

But Marshall, speaking for the Court, decided that a bank was necessary to the convenient transaction of the government's business. Since Congress could pass all laws necessary to enforcement of the Constitution, it could charter a bank. This is contrary to what he had said in *Marbury vs. Madison*.

Then he asserted that the fact that Congress considered a law allowing the Court to issue writs necessary to the convenient transaction of the Court's business did not give Congress the right to pass such a law. But in *McCulloch* there was no Cousin Tom to be slapped down, and Marshall never was one to worry too much about being consistent.

As to the second point, it was in this case that Marshall made his famous statement that "the power to tax is the power to destroy." He held that the Bank was an agency of the Federal government — rather a strained argument, since the government did not control it — so if the State had power to tax it, it had power to destroy an agency of the Federal government. If it could destroy one, why not all others? But to hold that one State could destroy the agencies of the Federal government was manifestly absurd. Therefore, the law was unconstitutional and void.

Some writers hold that this is the most important decision that John Marshall ever wrote. They say that it made the Federal government supreme over the States. Others are not so sure. They say that other decisions, long before *Marbury*, made the Federal power superior to the States. There is no manner of doubt, however, that John Marshall was tremendously important. He remained Chief Justice for thirty-four years, longer than any man, Chief or

Associate, has served on that bench, and he made the Court supreme in fact as well as in name.

To a large extent he did it by the very qualities that his enemies denounced. He was inconsistent. He could say one thing in *Marbury* and just the opposite in *McCulloch*. He was bold to the point of recklessness. In the Georgia Indian case he slammed headlong into prevailing public opinion and took a licking.

This was when the State of Georgia expelled certain Indians from lands granted them by treaty, but coveted by white settlers. President Andrew Jackson was an old Indian fighter and, like most frontiersmen, he had a low opinion of Indians. He approved the State's action, but when the case came before the Supreme Court, in 1832, Marshall ordered Georgia to restore the lands. Georgia paid not the slightest attention, and Jackson's enemies reported that he said, "John Marshall has made his decision; now let him enforce it." There is no proof that Jackson ever said it, but much evidence that it is what he thought, and public opinion throughout the country was behind Georgia rather than the Court; so its decision was of no effect.

In another case Marshall's decision was reversed by public opinion, although not until a long time afterward. In *Barron vs. Baltimore*, decided in 1833, he ruled that the Bill of Rights does not bind the

States. The Bill of Rights consists of the first ten
amendments of the Constitution, eight of which
name something that the government may not do
to a private citizen, as, for instance, abridge his freedom of speech, or establish a state religion. Marshall
held that such acts are forbidden to the Federal government, but not to the States. Thirty-five years later
the Fourteenth Amendment reversed this, declaring
that no State may deny the rights that men possess
as citizens of the United States.

Marshall was greedy for power. He denied Congress the right to extend the jurisdiction of the
Court, and then extended it himself many times farther than Congress ever meant to go. In fact, he
made the Supreme Court something that the men
who wrote the Constitution never imagined.

Generally speaking, a man who lets his personal
feelings influence his decisions is a bad judge, and
sometimes that applies to Marshall. His hatred of
Jefferson certainly influenced him in *Marbury,* and
even more when he presided over the trial of Aaron
Burr, accused of treason. There is no reason to believe that Marshall had any great love of Burr, but
Jefferson hated him and did everything he could
to get him hanged. That was enough to make Marshall determined that Burr should not hang. There
is all too much reason to believe that his desire to
spite Jefferson by freeing Burr made him define the

crime of treason so narrowly as to make it all but impossible to convict the mastermind who plans a treasonable act, unless he is fool enough to do the dirty work himself, instead of turning it over to his gunmen. Between them, Jefferson and Marshall did a great disservice to the United States in that case. This is the fact, although they were both great men.

John Marshall never retired. He died still Chief Justice at the age of eighty. Some people think that he would have resigned earlier except that in 1828, when he was seventy-three, a President was elected whom he hated even more violently than he hated Jefferson, and he wasn't going to give that man the satisfaction of naming a Chief Justice. This President was Andrew Jackson, and it was Marshall's last hope that when Jackson came up for re-election in 1832 he would be beaten by Henry Clay. But it didn't happen, so Marshall hung on, feeling sure that if he resigned Jackson would appoint Roger B. Taney (pronounced tawny), whom Marshall also despised. But he couldn't quite make it. In 1835, a year before the next election, he died and, just as he had feared, Jackson appointed Taney.

This Chief Justice made one terrible mistake, the Dred Scott decision, by which he very nearly wrecked the Supreme Court. So for many years he was regarded as a poor specimen and nobody, except a few specialists in legal history, gave him any serious study. But in recent years opinion has changed. It has changed so far that in 1961 one historian of the Supreme Court made the flat assertion that Taney was the second greatest Chief Justice, surpassed by Marshall alone.

This much, at least, is certain: before he tore it down, Taney built up the Supreme Court to a notable extent. But he did not work in the same way that Marshall did. Marshall was keenly aware most of the time that he had no physical force, no soldiers or policemen, to back up his decisions, and had to rely on public opinion alone. Some of his ideas, however, were far in advance of public opinion, and it was in connection with these that his great ability showed up. He was so clever a reasoner that he could take an obscure point of the law and make it so simple and plain that the ordinary citizen, who had never really thought about it at all, would be convinced that he had been thinking all along just as Marshall thought.

Taney's strength was different. Long experience in politics, much of it gained in working with that master politician, Andrew Jackson, had given him a remarkable ability to gauge popular opinion. Few men understood better how the average man would think about any proposal that might come up, and because he knew a great deal about the law, he could usually interpret it in a way that would agree with what the people were thinking. Marshall could make public opinion conform to the law. Taney could make the law conform to public opinion. But both of them kept the power of the nation behind the Court, and its prestige went up and up.

The dangerous failing of both men was a tendency to forget one tremendously important fact, namely, that government is not entirely law. In part it is policy, and only occasionally can policy be determined by law. When a problem comes up, if it is entirely a matter of law, the legislative and the judiciary, Congress and the Supreme Court, together can take care of it. But when it is a matter of policy, the legislative and the executive, Congress and the President, must handle it. The judiciary is out.

The Supreme Court can say what is constitutional, and what is in accord with the laws and customs of civilized nations. But it cannot say, when new conditions arise, what is best to do, what is expedient.

Although the Supreme Court has not a single bayonet or policeman's club with which to compel obedience to its decrees, its power is sufficient while it has public opinion behind it. Furthermore, as one great decision after another proved to be just and wise, the people's confidence in the Court rose steadily. Only when it undertook to decide what were really political questions — and how to deal with the Indians was largely a political question — was that confidence shaken. But Marshall's inclination was always to push the power of the Court as far as he could, and by the time of his death some sensible men were beginning to worry, for it seemed to them that the Court was trying to take over the whole government.

Then came Taney, and in his very first term he indicated that he would take a different line. It became plain in what is known as the Charles River Bridge case. The facts were that the State of Massachusetts had granted a charter to a company to build a toll bridge over the Charles River, to connect Boston and Cambridge. The tolls charged were high, but at first nobody objected. In the course of time, however, the company collected more than enough to repay it for what it had spent on the bridge, and people thought the tolls ought to be reduced. Not so the company. It continued to charge the same rate, which made its profits enormous. Finally the State decided to build a bridge of its own, which would be free of tolls and the company brought suit to stop it.

The company's argument was that if a toll bridge had a free bridge alongside it, everybody would take the free bridge and the toll bridge would become worthless. But the charter Massachusetts had issued was a contract by which the State was bound.

Such a contract implied that the State would do
nothing to destroy the value of the bridge. The Dartmouth College case had decided that a State may
not go back on its contract, so the Court was asked
to forbid the building of the free bridge.

Taney, speaking for the Court, said, yes, the charter was a contract, and the State must stick to it. But
there was not a word in the charter about a free
bridge. To say that an obligation not to build one
was implied by the charter would be to write something into the contract that was not in the original.
The State was bound by exactly what was written
there, not by anything that somebody might think
was implied. The State, therefore, could go ahead
and build the bridge.

Once again businessmen were tremendously re-
lieved, for Marshall had made a great deal of "implied powers" in the Constitution. This decision,
however, meant that the highest court would hold a
businessman bound by what was written in his contract, and by nothing else. Some had half expected
a ruling that there might be implied powers in a
business contract as well as in the Constitution. Now
businessmen were doubly reassured. The Dartmouth College case had settled that what is written
in a contract must be performed, even if a State is
one party. This new decision established that what
is not written in a contract need not be performed,

no matter how much someone thinks it ought to be.

This gave the businessman the feeling that he knew where he was. The decision came at a moment when it was needed, for in 1837, when it was rendered, what we call the Industrial Revolution was starting in a really big way in this country. It was making written contracts more numerous, more necessary, and more complicated, therefore trickier, than they had ever been before. As business increased, so did all the paper work connected with it, including contracts. As long as a man was doing business only with close neighbors whom he knew personally, he might rely on word-of-mouth agreements for some transactions. But when he dealt with strangers, or took on a big job that would last a long time, he needed a written contract. Thus a great many more people were interested in making contracts good in 1837 than had ever cared about them before.

For twenty years the Court under Chief Justice Taney followed the same course, not so much trying to extend its power as tightening its power by making the law clearer and more definite. As it did so, the prestige of the Court rose higher and higher, and people were less and less disposed to allow anybody to defy its rulings.

Now all this time, some say, there was one central question behind practically every case that came before the Supreme Court. The direct issue might be anything — contracts, or interstate commerce, or the Bank of the United States, or taxes, or what not — but behind the direct issue there was always the question of the relation of the various States to the Union.

At any rate, the great decisions of the Court under Marshall and Taney nearly all had to do with the relation of the States and the Union. Marshall, generally speaking, set the limits beyond which the States might not go; Taney, generally speaking, set the limits beyond which the Union might not go. Between them they clarified the law marvelously, and with such skill that to most of the people it seemed right and proper that the legal relation of State and Union should be as they said. So the Court came to be greatly respected and its power increased tremendously.

But government is not altogether law, and all this time in the political field tension was building up to the bursting point. The issue was Negro slavery, and it was actually a question, not of law, but of policy. The law was clear enough. The Constitution tolerated the institution of slavery, and the various laws relating to the subject were based on that toleration. But more and more people were coming to believe that the toleration itself was wrong. The remedy for that was amendment of the Constitution, but amendment is a matter of policy, not of law.

Taney's fatal error was in forgetting or ignoring this fact when the case of Dred Scott came before him. Scott was a slave in Missouri, who had been taken by his master into Illinois, where slavery was prohibited, and then returned to Missouri. After the return he sued for his freedom, arguing that when he was taken into a free State he automatically became free.

The way out for the Court was plain. Whatever he might have been in Illinois, under the laws of Missouri Scott was not a citizen, he was a slave with no standing in court, and it was from Missouri that he was suing. Again and again the Court had refused to interfere with the laws of a State regulating affairs within the State, and it could have denied-Dred Scott's contention by following those precedents.

But Taney chose not to do so. Instead of following the line the Court had taken in earlier cases, he tried to settle the question of slavery once and for all. He forgot or ignored that it wasn't a matter of law, it was a matter of policy. He made the Constitution, not the people, decide. He declared that Congress had no right whatever to interfere with slavery, and said that even the Missouri Compro-

mise, which Congress had passed thirty years earlier in an attempt to handle the slavery problem, was unconstitutional.

He made this ruling because of Articles Four and Six, and Amendment Ten, of the Constitution. Article Four compelled all States to recognize that a citizen of a slave state had a right to own slaves and that they were still his slaves when they ran away and escaped to a free state. Article Six says that the Constitution shall be the supreme law of the land. Amendment Ten says that any power not granted to the national government in the Constitution still belongs to the States. No power to abolish slavery had been granted to Congress, therefore that power belonged—was "reserved to"—the States and could not be exercised by Congress. More than that, Article Four commanded free States to hand over runaway slaves to their masters, and Congress could not change the Constitution. Therefore, it had no right to interfere with slavery and exceeded its powers when it tried to do so in the Missouri Compromise, which forbade slavery in any new State formed north of a certain line.

Even in 1787 many people disliked this part of the Constitution. You can tell by the way they avoided the words *slave* and *slavery*. You will not find them anywhere in the Constitution. The people of the United States were divided into three classes

— "free persons," "Indians not taxed," and "all other persons." Article Four doesn't call slaves by that name; they are "persons held to service or labor." But at the time it seemed to be necessary to recognize slavery or have no Constitution at all.

Of course, Taney was instantly denounced as a servile tool of the slaveowners. Thus the Court, up to that time more or less on the side lines, was thrown squarely into the midst of the controversy. The antislavery people suddenly found it their most formidable obstacle and attacked it furiously.

But Taney had never before been anybody's tool. True, he had helped Andrew Jackson destroy the Bank of the United States, but it was because he was convinced that the Bank ought to be destroyed, not because he was Jackson's lackey. So it seems likely that, as recent writers have suggested, he thought he was acting the patriot in the Dred Scott case. Like every other intelligent man, he saw that the quarrel was tearing the country apart. He saw, too, that although policy on this subject was disputed, the law was clear, and he made the mistake of thinking that by dragging the issue into the field of law he could settle it, and the country would be at peace.

He should have known better, because that is what Marshall thought in the case of the Georgia Indians, which was also a question of policy. When Marshall tried to drag it into the field of law, what he actually did was drag the Court into politics, where it was made to look ridiculous. But the case of the Indians was a minor one that did not agitate the whole country, so Marshall escaped with little more than a red face. Slavery, on the contrary, was the greatest issue then before the country, so when Taney dragged the Court into politics on that issue, he almost destroyed it and did wreck its prestige for years to come.

The cold fact was that people who thought about it at all had slowly been making up their minds that the system of human slavery was neither good morals nor good sense. George Washington owned slaves, and so did Thomas Jefferson, but they both worried about it. Neither thought that it was right for a man to own another man, as he owned a horse or a dog. They saw no way of getting rid of their slaves without upsetting the whole social system, but as early as 1776 they, and other wise men in the South as well as in the North, were sure that slavery was a bad system as far as morals were concerned.

Jefferson, in fact, wanted to write a paragraph denouncing it in the Declaration of Independence, but the other members of the committee, Adams, Franklin, Livingston, and Sherman, all Northerners, argued that it would start a row in the Continental Congress. They couldn't afford a split at that time, so they insisted that he leave it out. They were sure there would be a fight, because in 1776 most people were persuaded that there was money in the slave system; and when anything is believed to be profitable, it is easy for men to convince themselves that it is also right.

But by 1857, the date of the Dred Scott decision, many people had begun to doubt that slavery was really profitable. That very year Hinton Rowan Helper published *The Impending Crisis,* a book that tore to pieces the theory that the South was getting richer by employing slave labor. We know today that some of Helper's figures were wrong, and some of his arguments not sound, but in the main he was right. Slave labor may be profitable for a time in a strictly agricultural country, but it has never worked well in factories, and in the long run it doesn't even pay on the farm.

When the Supreme Court announced that a thing regarded by millions as both immoral and senseless could not be touched by any branch of the government, people did not respond by saying, "What a sacred thing is slavery!" They said, "What a silly thing is the Supreme Court!" Yet, as a matter of strict law, the Court was right. Under the law, slavery could not be touched. What Taney did not, and perhaps could not, realize was that this was no longer a question of law, having become a question of policy; and when the Court undertook to decide policy, it *was* silly.

Taney, thinking to bring about a peaceful settlement of the slavery question, really cut off the last hope of one. For when what most people regard as a great wrong exists, and they are told that nothing can be done about it peacefully, it is almost a certainty that something will be done about it violently.

That is the basic reason for the Civil War. The curious thing is that, at least in the beginning, people on both sides denied it. Lincoln himself said that he was fighting to preserve the Union, and if he could manage that without touching slavery, he would do it. The people of the South said they were not fighting for slavery, they were fighting for the sovereign rights of the States. Then there were other disputes — over the tariff, over taxation, over voting rights, and always the great division between country people and city people, between those who lived by farming and those who lived by factory work.

But all these were side issues. In time they could have been worked out without shedding blood. The fighting started because slavery had to go, and the Supreme Court said there was no way of getting rid of it by peaceful and orderly means, that is, by law. So the country got rid of it anyhow; but it took four

years of the bloodiest fighting in which Americans
have ever engaged, before or since. By the time it
was over laymen had decided that if the law couldn't
prevent that kind of thing, the law was not much
help.

How low the prestige of the Court sank is illustrated by the Merryman case. A man of that name
was picked up in Baltimore by the military police —
called in those day the "provost guard"—and thrown
into a cell at Fort McHenry for no real reason except
that some army officer had grown suspicious of him.
So Merryman's lawyer applied for a writ of *habeas
corpus.* That Latin term meaning, literally, "have
the body," is the name of an order that says the accused must be brought before a judge who can ex-
amine him and decide whether or not there is a good
reason for arresting him and bringing him to trial.
It means produce the man himself — *corpus,* "the
body" — not documents, or other objects that might
be evidence. "Have that man in court," says the
order, the idea being that he will then have a chance
to speak for himself.

Any judge of a state court, or any Federal district
judge, can issue a writ of *habeas corpus.* In this case,
however, Chief Justice Taney went from Washington to Baltimore and signed the writ himself. But the
commandant in the fort not only refused to produce
the prisoner, he would not even accept the writ, say-

ing that he was acting under the orders of the President and would recognize no other authority. And nothing was done about it.

When any man, military officer or any other, can refuse to accept, much less obey, an order signed by the Chief Justice of the United States, and not be punished for it, regard for the Court has sunk very low indeed. Not even Marshall, in the case of the Georgia Indians, had been so directly humiliated.

The fact is that laymen felt that the Court had failed them. In the great crisis it had proved to be strictly a court of law, not, as laymen thought it should be, a court of justice. The law, thinks the layman, is intended to serve justice, but it doesn't always do so. It may be because the men who wrote the law were stupid and phrased it badly. More often it is because conditions have changed to such an extent that what seemed just and right when the law was enacted has now become plainly unjust and wrong. The lower courts may feel that they, being strictly courts of law, have no authority to take this into consideration, but somewhere in the judicial system there should be an interpreter, who can construe the law so as to serve the ends of justice, for justice is what we must assume the legislature intended to achieve.

It comes to this: while the Constitution is the supreme law of the land, the supreme power of the

land is the will of the majority, "which to be rightful," said Jefferson, "must be reasonable," but which,
rightful or not, "is in all cases to prevail." In any
particular case, such as slavery, the reasonableness
of the will of the majority is determined, not by law,
but by public opinion. That is to say, it is a political
not a legal problem.

When the Supreme Court undertakes to decide a
political issue, it is taking a very serious risk. If it
decides against the will of the majority, its power
vanishes. In spite of the Supreme Court, the Indians
were thrown out of Georgia. In spite of the Supreme
Court, slavery was destroyed. Today most people
believe that in the case of the Indians the will of the
majority was unreasonable and wrongful, and in the
case of slavery just the opposite. But in both cases it
prevailed, and the Supreme Court was made to look
foolish.

For this reason Roger B. Taney has come down
in history as at best a second-rate character, although he was actually a better lawyer than John
Marshall, and almost as great a judge. But he gave
the wrong answer to a critical question and that
made the country forget all his earlier good work.

It is a fact, though, that Marshall and Taney between them led the movement that brought the Supreme Court from the position of a rather unimpor-
tant agency to that of the third branch of the govern-

ment, standing on a level with Congress and the President, and having in many respects greater dignity than either. Of course, the Chief Justices merely led. They had many distinguished Associates, who did much of the work of building up the institution; but people will always refer to "the Marshall Court" and "the Taney Court," because it is convenient and something more. There is a distinction between the Courts that is quite real. They gave different answers to the great question that lay behind every important decision they made — "In what respects and how much is the Nation greater than the States?" Marshall pushed the power of the Federal government as far as he could. Taney set limits beyond which it should not go. They balanced each other, and together they made the Supreme Court really the third power of government, which it had not been in the earliest days.

"Equal Justice Under Law"

THE CIVIL WAR settled forever the main question about the relation of the States and the Union. Every year minor questions still come up, but the war gave the final answer to the main one. It proved that the Union is dominant over the States and that the Constitution and the laws made by Congress under it are the supreme law of the land, regardless of what any state legislature may do. As lawyers say, "the writ of the Supreme Court runs" in every part of the country, and it is the President's duty to enforce that writ, no matter what any state court may say.

But once that question was decided, another immediately took its place. It is, "What is the relation of the Union to the men and women who compose the States?" This question has been behind every important decision of the Court since Taney, but for a short time it seemed that the Court would have no voice in answering it. Right after the end of the Civil War Congress tried to take over everything.

It was due to war fever, which always runs highest just after the artillery has fallen silent. There is a remark that, "Americans never get mad until the war's over." It isn't true, but sometimes it looks that way, because while the fighting is on we are too busy to give much attention to the hatreds and malice and spite that war always arouses. As soon as the firing ceases, however, these things break out.

Right after the Civil War Lincoln, who had fought to save the Union, intended to restore it as rapidly as possible, and to that end he wanted the victorious North to forgive and forget. But Lincoln was murdered, and Andrew Johnson, the Vice-President, although honest and brave, was no Lincoln. To induce people who have just been through a terrible fight to forgive and forget takes a very great man. It is not certain that Lincoln could have done it, and poor Johnson never had a chance. When he tried to carry out Lincoln's policy the radical element in Congress accused him of trying to cheat the North out of its victory, and the country almost believed it.

That brought the prestige of the Presidency to a very low ebb. Since the Dred Scott decision had already hurt the prestige of the Supreme Court, it looked as if this was a fine opportunity for Congress to take over all power and bring this country to something like the British parliamentary system. Certain members of Congress, led by Thaddeus Stevens in the House and Charles Sumner in the Senate, tried to do it and came very near succeeding. For one thing, they brought a bill of impeachment against President Johnson.

The word *impeach* means *accuse*, but to accuse in a formal way by certain authorities. In the case of the President, the House of Representatives may impeach him, but he cannot be removed until the House has proved that he is guilty — in the words of the Constitution—"of treason, bribery, or other high crimes and misdemeanors." The Chief Justice of the United States is to be the judge, and the Senate is to be the jury. No President shall be convicted unless two thirds of the Senators vote that he is guilty.

Taney had died in 1864 and Salmon P. Chase was now Chief Justice. He presided over the trial. Chase, who had been Secretary of the Treasury under Lincoln and wanted to be President, was regarded as more of a politician than a judge, and there were some who expected him to be all politician on this occasion, siding with Stevens and Sumner, who certainly had the mob with them. But Chase saw clearly that there would not be much left of either the Chief Justice or the President if Congress took over everything. More than that, he was a good enough lawyer to see that the charges against the President were

flimsy, and he thought Stevens and Sumner were playing the fool to try to impeach him with no better case.

So Chase determined that as far as he was concerned the trial was going to be a fair trial conducted according to the long-established rules. And that was what he made it. As one charge after another was brought against Johnson, he made the accusers prove it, or try to, and he would not admit mere gossip as proof. He allowed the President's lawyers to cross-examine witnesses, and again and again they showed that the witness knew nothing, that he was merely repeating rumors. Eventually it became plain that all his enemies really had against Johnson was that they didn't like him.

Nobody believed that he was guilty of treason or bribery, but they tried to get him under "other high crimes and misdemeanors." What it came down to was that he had removed the Secretary of War, although Congress didn't want him removed. That, said the accusers, meant that he had violated the Constitution although he had sworn to defend it, and when a President breaks his oath, that is a high crime and a misdemeanor. When the vote came thirty-five Senators voted "guilty," but nineteen voted "not guilty." Out of a total of fifty-four it took thirty-six to make two thirds, and they had only thirty-five. So Johnson escaped conviction by one

vote. Later he was elected a member of the very
Senate that had tried him, which shows what the
people of his own state, Tennessee, thought of him.
Yet if Chase had not been scrupulously fair, the
President would almost certainly have been con-
victed and removed.

At first the Chief Justice was violently abused for
being fair, but in a little while, after passions began
to cool and men had time to think it over, opinion
changed. It was realized that if Andrew Johnson had
actually been removed from office, because Congress
didn't like him, no President thereafter would have
dared stand up against Congress; and most Americans thought that would be a bad thing. They don't
want the man in the White House to be afraid of
anything, certainly not of either of the other branches
of government.

And the President's removal had been prevented
by the Chief Justice. When the law commanded him
to preside at an impeachment trial, he presided, and
he allowed nobody else to run that court, Congress
included. Some people who had had a low opinion
of the Court ever since the Dred Scott decision
found themselves thinking it a pretty good thing,
after all, to have one tribunal that nobody could
scare. Some who thoroughly disliked Johnson came
to see that ruining the prestige of the office would
be worse than letting a bad President serve out his

term, and they were thankful to Chase for the way he had run the trial.

So this Chief Justice, merely by doing his duty, went far toward restoring the people's high opinion of the Court. As time passed his conduct looked better and better, and in the course of a few years most Americans decided that the Court had never been what its enemies called it. Even Taney's ruinous decision, although wrong, was rendered because he thought it was right, not because he had been bribed or scared into making it. So the Court gradually regained its old standing.

But the lesson was not lost upon the justices. For the next fifty years the Court was careful to decide the exact point of law that was before it, and nothing more. Many times cases came up on appeal in which the lawyers argued that the judge in the lower court made the wrong ruling and, in addition to that, the law in question was unconstitutional. In such a case, if the Supreme Court found that the judge of the lower court had in fact made a wrong ruling, the case was decided on that point alone, and nothing was said about the constitutionality of the law. The Court was determined never to strike down an act of Congress if the case before it could be justly decided without doing so. That is to say, it was sticking to law and avoiding policy. As it did, its prestige rose higher and higher.

Now the Supreme Court began to use its voice to answer the question of the relation of the country to the individual citizen. At this time the individual citizen meant, first of all, the businessman, so it is natural that for a long time nearly all the important decisions of the Court had something to do with how business and the government were to get along with each other.

After 1865 the country was in a condition that made the businessman all-important. The Civil War had left the South completely ruined, and the North not much better off. Nearly all the savings the people had been accumulating for a hundred years were gone—turned into gunpowder and burnt, or into bullets and shells and shot away, or into food and clothing consumed by the armies. Half a million strong young men had been killed, and many more crippled for life. An enormous national debt had been incurred.

In a situation like that, a man who knows how to run a money-making enterprise — that is, a business-man — is about the most important man a country can have. Everything else, except money, we had. Our continent was one of the richest in the world in raw materials. But coal and iron do nobody any good while they are buried in the ground, and they don't come up of themselves. Forests don't saw themselves into lumber. Wheat and corn and cotton,

hogs and cattle, don't carry themselves to the markets where they are needed. Organizing men to dig
the coal and iron, to build and run the railroads, to
manage the weaving mills and grain elevators and
livestock markets, was the first job; and it was the
job of the businessman.

So it was plain good sense to get out of the businessman's way and let him do his stuff, just as everyone gets out of the soldier's way in time of war. That
is what this country did. And the businessmen did a
tremendous job in those years. When they began,
the whole country west of the Mississippi River was
for the most part empty. But by 1893 the government could formally declare that the frontier, that
is, the edge of civilization, no longer existed. It had
been pushed to the Pacific Ocean.

And what about the Supreme Court in those
days? Why, it was traveling along, not too far ahead
of public opinion, not too far behind it. In general,
it accepted the idea prevailing all over the country
that business ought to be encouraged, not discour-
aged, by the interpreters of the law. In later years,
when it became plain that this idea had resulted in
some pretty bad decisions, liberals were inclined to
say that the Court, like the rest of the country, was
living through a period of very low morals when the
worst sort of actions, even including downright
stealing, were admired if they made money.

But that was probably not true either of the country or the Court. Although some of its decisions did give some men an unfair advantage over others, the Court was acting for what it honestly believed was the general welfare. The need to rebuild the country after the Civil War wasn't any fairy tale, it was hard fact. The scheme of occupying and developing the empty land in the West wasn't an idle dream, it was a first-rate business proposition. Businessmen were doing both, effectively and rapidly. Why shouldn't the Court encourage them? It did.

It did some other things, too, that ought not to be forgotten. As early as 1866, in a case called by lawyers *Ex parte Milligan*, it asserted once more its sole right to judge civilians, and this time made it stick, unlike the Merryman case. A man named Lambdin P. Milligan, of Indiana, was arrested there, tried by a military court, and sentenced to hang. There is grave doubt that Merryman was guilty of any crime, but there is hardly any doubt that Milligan was guilty of high treason. He had conspired to overthrow the lawful government of Indiana and make peace with the Confederacy.

But although the war was going on at the time of the conspiracy, the actual fighting was a long way from Indiana. The regular courts, both State and Federal, were open in Indiana and were trying cases as usual. They were perfectly capable of dealing

with any crime, including treason. Military courts were to try soldiers for military offenses. They had no business trying civilians as long as the civil courts were there and doing business as usual. Hence the judgment of the Supreme Court was that the military court should not have tried Milligan, and Milligan should not hang. He didn't. Since then it has been accepted doctrine that as long as a civil court is open, a civilian must be tried there, and not by a court-martial.

In general, though, the important decisions from 1865 to 1900 were in the line of preventing interference with the businessman in his great task of building up the country. As time passed, however, some businessmen began to use the great powers granted them not to build up the country, but to tear down their rivals, and, especially, to hold down their employees. Then these decisions were seen in a different light. Men began to think, and say, that what the Court was most interested in protecting was money, and they grew more and more bitter about it.

In 1873 the Court ruled, in the Slaughterhouse case, that a State may grant a monopoly to certain businesses; in 1886 it ruled that a corporation is a "person" within the meaning of the Fourteenth Amendment; in 1890 it held that the courts can upset any state rate regulation that they find unreasonable; in 1895 it held that the anti-trust law did not apply to monopolies in manufacturing; and the same year it decided that an income tax was unconstitutional.

By 1895 public opinion was getting well ahead of the Court. Farmers and factory workers were saying that, after all, the businessman is not the only person in the community with rights worth protecting. Perhaps even more effective in making these decisions unpopular was the fact that big business was no longer conducted by individual businessmen, but by corporations.

There is a great difference in public opinion. A powerful and energetic man is admired for his power and energy, even by those who do not like what he is doing. When he shows courage as well, he is very much admired. For instance, when Commodore Vanderbilt ran head-on into the Fulton-Livingston steamboat monopoly, many felt bound to hurrah for the nerve of the man, even though they thought he was being too rough about it. But nobody gets enthusiastic over a committee, and a corporation is a committee. There is no personal bravery in a corporation.

Long before this country was founded, English law had provided for the way of doing business that is called corporative. Three or more men might agree to join in some enterprise — to build a factory, perhaps, or to set up a store, or a bank, or anything else — and to get the thing going each would contribute a certain amount of money to the capital stock, with the understanding that profits of the business would be shared in the same way. The man who contributed one fourth of the capital stock would get one fourth of the profits, and so on. Then they would apply for a charter to do the kind of business they had in mind, and when the charter was issued the business became a corporation, a word going back to the Latin *corpus,* "a body."

Men can agree to do business together merely as partners, without becoming a corporation, but in that case if the business fails each partner is responsible for all its debts. If a corporation fails, the stockholders lose what money they have put into it but, except in a few special cases, no more. Once the charter is issued the corporation becomes, in the eyes of the law, somebody, in the sense that it may own, buy, and sell property, sue and be sued in the courts, and do whatever else is necessary to carry on the business for which it is chartered, just as if it were one man, not a group. A man is called a natural person. This "legal fiction," the corporation, is called a juristic person. But in legal language they are both persons.

Now the Fourteenth Amendment, as everybody agrees, was adopted to protect the rights of the newly emancipated slaves. For that purpose it contains these words: "No State shall . . . deprive any person of life, liberty, or property without due process of law, nor deny to any person within its jurisdiction the equal protection of the laws." There is no doubt whatever that Congress, in submitting this amendment, had Negroes in mind, but in 1887 the Supreme Court ruled that a person is a person, juristic or natural, so the words applied to corporations as well as to former slaves.

It is plain to see that you can't deprive a legal fiction of life or liberty, since it has neither, but you can deprive it of property; yet not, says the amendment, "without due process of law."

What, then, is "due process of law?" American lawyers have been arguing that question ever since 1887, and will continue to argue it, for there are several answers, most of them highly complicated.

One answer is simple enough. It is that "due process" means going through the prescribed motions. For instance, if a man owes you money and will not pay, although he is rich, you cannot simply go over and seize as much of his property as will meet the debt. You must bring suit, and from the court get a written order called a judgment. You then turn the judgment over to the sheriff, or other officer as the law provides, who will then seize any of the debtor's property that he can find, sell it, and hand the money to the clerk of the court. Out of this money the clerk will thereupon pay you what is your due. That is one meaning of due process of law.

It is also part of what the Fourteenth Amendment means, but there is a general feeling that it isn't all that it means, that life and liberty were the important things in the minds of the men who wrote the amendment. Reasonable people feel that if you are about to take away a man's life, or his liberty, it is not enough to get the proper paper served by the proper officer and do all the other things in the correct fashion. Over and above all that, it is necessary to have a reason for acting that the law will recognize as a good reason. Without that reason, you do not have due process.

When the Court began to apply this argument to corporations, there were sharp differences of opinion as to what is a sound reason for depriving a corporation of property. In case after case the Court seemed to take the position that an act of Congress may be deemed unconstitutional if, in the opinion of the Court, it seemed an unreasonable interference with business. But these decisions began to edge out of the field of law over into that of policy; and court decisions involving policy are judge-made law of the riskiest kind.

There were always some justices who realized this and wrote dissents that afterward, sometimes many years afterward, were recognized as being better law than the majority decision. One such was Edward D. White, appointed by President Cleveland, in 1894, and made Chief Justice by President Taft in 1910. He came from Louisiana and had been a Confederate soldier in the Civil War, so when a Republican President — White was a Democrat — made him Chief Justice, people said that at last the war was really over.

In 1902 Oliver Wendell Holmes joined the Court, in 1910 Charles E. Hughes, and in 1916 Louis D. Brandeis, all of them great judges and all determined to protect American freedom. All found themselves overruled sometimes and wrote dissents that have become famous. It became almost a regular thing for the newspapers to announce that the Supreme Court had decided thus-and-so, "Holmes and Brandeis dissenting." This meant that Associate Justice Oliver Wendell Holmes and Associate Justice Louis D. Brandeis had thought that the other seven justices were wrong, and had stated their reasons for so thinking. Now Holmes and Brandeis were very great judges, with extraordinary ability to see into the future. More than once it happened that within a year, or within two or three years, something would come up to prove that they had been right. It happened so often that the thing became almost a joke, and men would say, "Well, the decision is the other way, but if you want to know the rights of the matter, read the dissents."

In the first years after the Civil War the country thought pretty much as the Court thought, and few seriously questioned its decisions. But when the war had been over twenty-five years, the mood of the country began to change. By 1890 the physical damage done by the war had been repaired, and from then on it did not seem so necessary to make everybody and everything else stand back in order to give the businessman a free hand.

Shifts in public opinion, however, are always slow to affect the Court, and this one did not make much impression until about 1900. In 1901 Theodore Roosevelt became President, and he and the Court did not get along very well. Roosevelt thought that some of the great business corporations were getting too strong for the good of the country, and he wanted to crack down on them. This was the policy that the newspapers of the time called "trust busting." But the Supreme Court was less enthusiastic about trust busting. In one famous decision, the Northern Securities case, it did forbid the principal railroads of the Northwest to join in one company. But in general it was inclined to go slowly, so slowly that at one time Roosevelt wanted it made possible for judicial decisions to be recalled by vote of the people.

The first Roosevelt didn't get very far with his schemes to control business, and the next President, Taft, didn't try. With the election of Woodrow Wilson, in 1912, however, the Court finally began to feel the force of the change of thinking in the country, but this influence did not last long, for in 1914 World War I broke out, and after that everyone was thinking more about defending the country than about improving its legal system.

It was the panic of 1929 and the depression following it that set us to doing some really hard thinking about our form of government. The shock was so terrific that for more than three years nobody in this country seemed to know what to do. By that time a second Roosevelt, a distant cousin of the first one, had been elected President, and he hit the nail on the head. True, he didn't know any more about how to rebuild the economic system than anybody else, but he knew what was at the bottom of the trouble. It was that we had gone on too long thinking that "the people" meant the businessman first, and everybody else a long time afterward. It had been true at one time, but it was no longer true when Franklin D. Roosevelt became President.

Yet while this was clear to the President, it wasn't

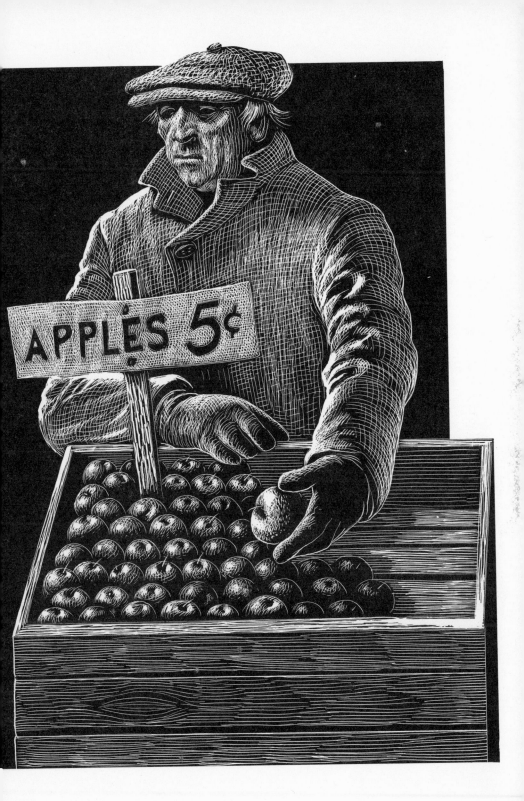

at all clear to some others, among whom were at least five members of the Supreme Court. So when the President proposed a policy of thinking about the people with no money and no jobs first, and about businessmen later, businessmen naturally thought that Roosevelt was their enemy, and their friends agreed.

The outcome was a series of tremendous political battles, and the Supreme Court was in the middle of the fight. Perhaps to say "in the middle" is wrong, because the Supreme Court never gets into the beginning of a fight. The fight begins in the lower courts, State or Federal, and gets to the Supreme Court only after it has been fought out in the lower courts and the losing side has appealed from the decision. It may start in a Federal district court in one of the States; then it has to go to the circuit Court of Appeals whose circuit includes that State; and only after it has been heard twice does it get to the Supreme Court.

This process takes months, often years, so not until 1935 and 1936 did the Supreme Court begin to get the important cases under the laws passed by Congress to support Roosevelt's policy of encouraging the people first and business later — the policy commonly known as the New Deal. But when the big cases did come up, the Supreme Court struck down the New Deal laws one after another, usually by a vote of five to four. Chief Justice Hughes and Associate Justices Brandeis, Cardozo, and Stone saw Roosevelt's point. While they did not altogether agree with the President — Hughes was very doubtful — they felt that these matters were ones of political policy rather than of constitutional law, and policy is in the hands of the President and Congress. So they usually voted to sustain the laws.

The other five, however, couldn't see it that way at all, and they steadily voted to strike down the New Deal laws. When four of the most important had been knocked out, it seemed likely that Roosevelt and Congress could get nothing done. The executive and the legislative branches were helpless.

Then in 1936 Roosevelt was re-elected by such a tremendous majority that only the States of Maine and Vermont voted against him. If he had not been persuaded before, this proved to the Chief Justice that the Court was far out of line with public opinion, and he knew what that meant. He remembered Taney and the Dred Scott decision.

The President, of course, was enraged, and after the election of 1936 he resolved to ask Congress for a law enabling him to enlarge the Court from nine to fifteen members. With four who favored the New Deal already on the Court, six new members also favorable would constitute a majority of ten to five. As a matter of fact, he needed only one more favorable vote, and while the bill was still before Congress, Hughes gave him that one. He persuaded Associate Justice Roberts to accept Hughes' view that these laws were actually matters of policy and, therefore, should not be rejected by the Court. When the fifth big case came up, Roberts voted to sustain the law — it was the Agricultural Adjustment Act — and that made the decision five to four in favor of the New Deal.

With that, the steam went out of the drive to enlarge — Roosevelt's enemies said "to pack" — the Court, and Congress voted the bill down. But there is little doubt that the real victory was won by Chief Justice Hughes. He prevented another mistake like the one that Taney had made, and so prevented another collapse of the Court's prestige to the low point it had touched under Taney.

The fact remains, though, that when he touched the Court, Roosevelt suffered a tremendous defeat. This is impressive, because he was the most popular President of all time, as is shown not only by the election of 1936, but by his re-election in 1940, and, for a fourth time, in 1944. If Roberts had not switched, the bill enlarging the Court probably would have gone through — giving the wits a chance to say, "a switch in time saves nine." But without a very powerful reason for tampering with the Court, even the popularity of a Roosevelt is unable to overcome its prestige. Roberts removed the reason, and from that moment Roosevelt was whipped.

So the fact that the Court does not, as a rule, accept the most advanced social and political ideas becomes a bad thing only when the Court falls too far behind. Experience has shown, indeed, that there is nearly always on the Court one man, and often two or three, whose ideas are far in advance of majority opinion. In recent years it has become common to read after the announcement of a decision, "Douglas and Black dissenting." Mr. Justice Douglas and Mr. Justice Black have not been proved right as often as Holmes and Brandeis, but neither has as much time passed since they filed their dissents, for they are still on the Court. In time they may rank with the other two.

In any event, when the United States Supreme Court passes on a difficult point of law, the correct solution of the difficulty is nearly always to be found in either the majority decision or in the dissents. That is why the Supreme Court, although it is frequently abused and occasionally overruled by the people, has commanded their respect in an increasing degree until today, without a single soldier's bayonet, or a single policeman's club to back it, it is the most powerful tribunal in the world.

But its power is still far from absolute. That was proved in 1954 when the Court reversed its own decision in the Plessy case and declared that racial segregation in the public schools violated the Fourteenth Amendment. Seven years after that decision two states were still refusing to accept it and fifteen others had accepted it with no enthusiasm, several so grudgingly as to make it no more than token acceptance.

This shows the danger of making any positive statement about the place of the Supreme Court in our system of government. Should the Court rule in the field of law and leave the field of policy to the other branches of the government? That is a question that has bothered all students of the Court and completely baffled most of them. For the truth is, you can't separate law and policy entirely. Some things are clearly one or the other, but many others come up at the point where law and policy mix and mingle to such an extent that you can't tell which is one and which the other.

Segregation is such a matter. To compel people to associate when they don't like each other is certainly to deny their right to the pursuit of happiness, and most of us think it a denial of liberty as well; and the Declaration of Independence says that liberty and the pursuit of happiness are inalienable rights.

On the other hand, a war that almost destroyed the nation forced us to take the stand that no State shall deny "to any person within its jurisdiction the equal protection of the laws." Most certainly school children are persons, and most certainly public schools are established by law. If *separate* means *unequal*, then children forced by law into separate schools are not given the equal protection of the laws.

The Supreme Court decided that people's right to equal protection of the laws is more important than their right to choose those with whom they will associate. Most Americans agree that the Court was right, but not all, and those who disagree feel bitter about it.

In three different cases coming up to the Supreme Court from various places, the lower courts had decided, following Plessy, that "separate but equal" schools met the requirement of equal protection of the laws. But the plaintiffs appealed, contending that if schools were separate they could not be equal, and the Supreme Court decided that it was true. The law remained precisely what it was in 1896. The difference was that the theory of "separate but equal" had been tried for fifty-eight years and hadn't worked, so it appeared to the Court that if it couldn't be made to work in fifty-eight years it couldn't be made to work at all, which meant that the theory must be false. Neither Congress nor the Court can make true what is plainly not true, and when they try, the result is bad law. The real meaning of the 1954 segregation decision is simply that the Court refused any longer to pretend that this belief, widely held in 1896, could be believed in 1954.

The great error of Taney in the Dred Scott decision was that he didn't allow for the influence of time on public opinion. If he had rendered that decision in 1806 instead of 1856, the chances are that it would have been accepted as the Plessy decision was accepted in 1896. But in fifty years a majority of the people had changed their minds about slavery, as they changed their minds about segregation by 1954. The whole power of the Supreme Court rests upon the belief of a majority that its decisions are, on the whole, reasonable and right.

It is exceedingly important for all Americans to understand this, because within the next few years the country — and therefore the Court — must make a great many decisions that are sure to strain our wisdom to the limit. This is bound to happen, because the world is changing very rapidly. There was a time when the average American believed — when he thought about it at all — that there would always be slaves because there always had been slaves. We didn't grasp what it meant when the civilized nations in the rest of the world, from Great Britain even to Russia, began to abolish slavery, or serfdom, a slightly better form of slavery. We thought that what they did didn't affect us.

Even when by the dreadful means of civil war we had done away with slavery, we thought for a long time that the way we arranged for the races to live together was strictly our own affair. So, indeed, it seemed until quite recently. But since World War II the colored races, of whom there are a great many more than there are of the white, have begun to win their independence. The white races are no longer strong enough to hold them down, and the wiser white men have learned that holding other races down is not worth what it costs anyhow.

This complicated the segregation issue. We learned that the colored nations in the rest of the world regarded segregation as wrong and insulting. More than that, in a nation that claimed to be democratic, it seemed hypocritical; so it was giving the United States a bad name.

We boast of American liberty, but we never have claimed that it includes liberty to inflict damage on the country knowingly and willfully. Minorities have their rights, which "to violate," said Jefferson, "would be oppression." But what minority has a right to pursue a course that is hurtful and dangerous to the whole country? There is a question for the Supreme Court, and a thorny one it is.

It came up in connection with segregation, and

it is going to come up in an unknown number of other things. Therefore, Americans ought to be prepared for a long series of decisions that may startle us, because they are based on new, or newly discovered, facts to which we had not paid enough attention. But if we, the people, do not realize that such decisions are in fact reasonable and right, much of the effective power of the Court will be lost; and unless the Court remains powerful its ideal, "Equal justice under law," will never be attained.

We have had a glimpse of this danger since the segregation decision of 1954. A great many Americans had their doubts about it, but most of them had confidence enough in the Court to be willing to accept it and see how it worked out. But some were so infuriated and so confident of the rightness of their own view that they denounced the Court, and a few went so far as to advocate impeaching all nine justices.

That, of course, is the wrong way to go about it. If the decison was, in fact, wrong and unreasonable, there is a way to overrule it. That way is to adopt an amendment to the Constitution legalizing segregation. It was done with regard to the income tax, which the Court declared unconstitutional just a year before the Plessy decision. In 1913 the Sixteenth Amendment made it constitutional, and that was that.

But the men who screamed most loudly that the justices had violated their oath and should be impeached were doing so because they knew very well that they could never get an amendment through; a majority of Americans wouldn't stand for it. Therefore, they hoped by threatening the justices to force them to the opposite point of view. This is the very reverse of Americanism, which holds that judges must be bound by nothing except the law and the truth, and that to compel them by threats to decide otherwise is criminal.

The Supreme Court usually represents American intelligence at its best. The care with which Presidents make appointments assures us always of good judges, and sometimes of great judges. But as water can never rise above its source, so the thinking of the Supreme Court can never be better than the best American thinking about public affairs. If, as sometimes happens, even intelligent Americans allow themselves to be overwhelmed by popular enthusiasm for some trumpery delusion, or by a popular fear of some bogy, and if that pressure continues for a considerable time, then it is highly probable that the thinking of the Court will come to be worse than the best.

Thus it happens that the Court, for all its dignity and its separation from the hurly-burly of business and politics, is, like the President and Congress, a sort of mirror of the state of the nation. No Court, constituted as this one is, can remain independent of public opinion for more than a relatively short time. As you and I and millions like us think, so, in the course of time, will the Court think. For it is part of the nation, and a nation that allows itself to be swept by panic, or by national hatred, or by national greed, or by baseless prejudice, will never for any length of time have a great Court. A great Court cannot exist without a great nation to sustain it.

Justices of the United States Supreme Court

(*) indicates Chief Justice

Name	Term	Name	Term
*John Jay	1789-1795	Smith Thompson	1823-1843
John Rutledge	1789-1791	Robert Trimble	1826-1828
William Cushing	1789-1810	John McLean	1829-1861
James Wilson	1789-1798	Henry Baldwin	1830-1844
John Blair	1789-1796	James M. Wayne	1835-1867
Robert H. Harrison	1789-1790	*Roger B. Taney	1836-1864
James Iredell	1790-1799	Philip P. Barbour	1836-1841
Thomas Johnson	1791-1793	John Catron	1837-1865
William Paterson	1793-1806	John McKinley	1837-1852
*John Rutledge	1795-1795	Peter V. Daniel	1841-1860
Samuel Chase	1796-1811	Samuel Nelson	1845-1872
*Oliver Ellsworth	1796-1799	Levi Woodbury	1845-1851
Bushrod Washington	1798-1829	Robert C. Grier	1846-1870
Alfred Moore	1799-1804	Benjamin R. Curtis	1851-1857
*John Marshall	1801-1835	John A. Campbell	1853-1861
William Johnson	1804-1834	Nathan Clifford	1858-1881
Brockholst Livingston	1806-1823	Noah H. Swayne	1862-1881
Thomas Todd	1807-1826	Samuel F. Miller	1862-1890
Joseph Story	1811-1845	David Davis	1862-1877
Gabriel Duval	1812-1835	Stephen J. Field	1863-1897

Name	Term	Name	Term
*Salmon P. Chase	1864-1873	Louis D. Brandeis	1916-1939
William Strong	1870-1880	John H. Clarke	1916-1922
Joseph P. Bradley	1870-1892	*William H. Taft	1921-1930
Ward Hunt	1873-1882	George Sutherland	1922-1938
*Morrison R. Waite	1874-1888	Pierce Butler	1922-1939
John M. Harlan	1877-1911	Edward T. Sanford	1923-1930
William B. Woods	1881-1887	Harlan F. Stone	1925-1941
Stanley Matthews	1881-1889	*Charles E. Hughes	1930-1941
Horace Gray	1882-1902	Owen J. Roberts	1930-1945
Samuel Blatchford	1882-1893	Benjamin N. Cardozo	1932-1938
Lucius Q. C. Lamar	1888-1893	Hugo L. Black	1937-
*Melville W. Fuller	1888-1910	Stanley F. Reed	1938-1957
David J. Brewer	1889-1910	Felix Frankfurter	1939-
Henry B. Brown	1890-1906	William O. Douglas	1939-
George Shiras, Jr.	1892-1903	Frank Murphy	1940-1949
Howell E. Jackson	1893-1895	*Harlan F. Stone	1941-1946
Edward D. White	1894-1910	James F. Byrnes	1941-1942
Rufus W. Peckham	1896-1909	Robert H. Jackson	1941-1954
Joseph McKenna	1898-1925	Wiley B. Rutledge	1943-1949
Oliver W. Holmes	1902-1932	Harold H. Burton	1945-1958
William R. Day	1903-1922	*Fred M. Vinson	1946-1953
William H. Moody	1906-1910	Tom C. Clark	1949-
Horace H. Lurton	1910-1914	Sherman Minton	1949-1956
Charles E. Hughes	1910-1916	*Earl Warren	1953-
Willis Van Devanter	1910-1937	John Marshall Harlan	1955-
Joseph R. Lamar	1911-1916	William J. Brennan, Jr.	1956-
*Edward D. White	1910-1921	Charles E. Whittaker	1957-1962
Mahlon Pitney	1912-1922	Potter Stewart	1958-
James C. McReynolds	1914-1941	Byron R. White	1962-

Index